"The Little Bug Catcher"

by Grandma Susie

I really like bugs. Do you?

I look for bugs everyday.

You can find them in the grass, on the sidewalk, or in a tree when you play.

They are everywhere!
Just look and see...

I catch the bugs and put them in my bug cage where they are safe and can breathe.

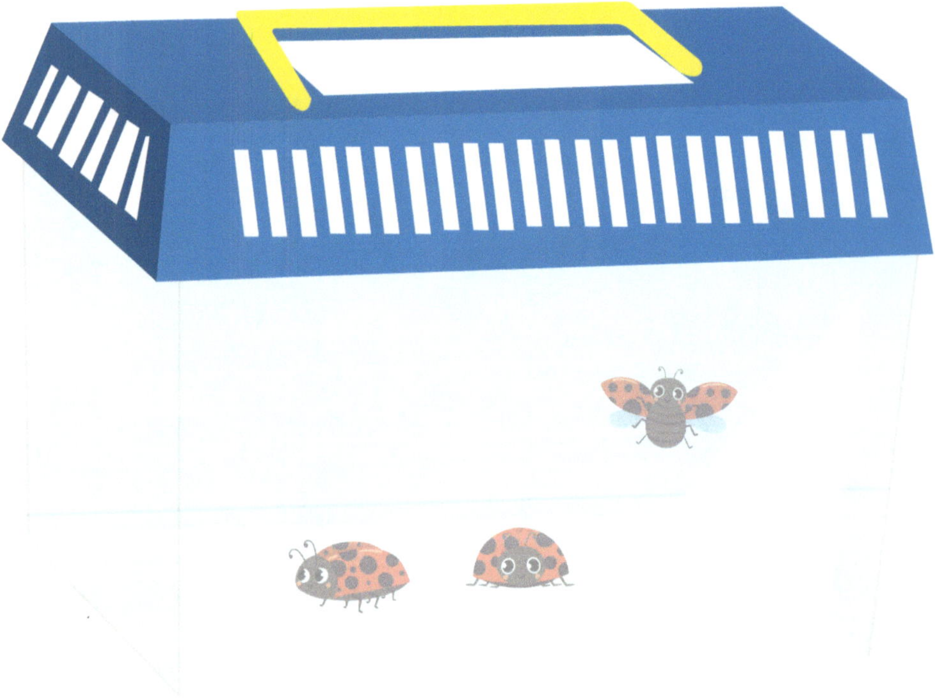

I also have a magnifying glass that makes

little, tiny bugs look really, really BIG!

I use special tweezers to catch the bugs...
They have little cups
So, I can scoop the bugs up!

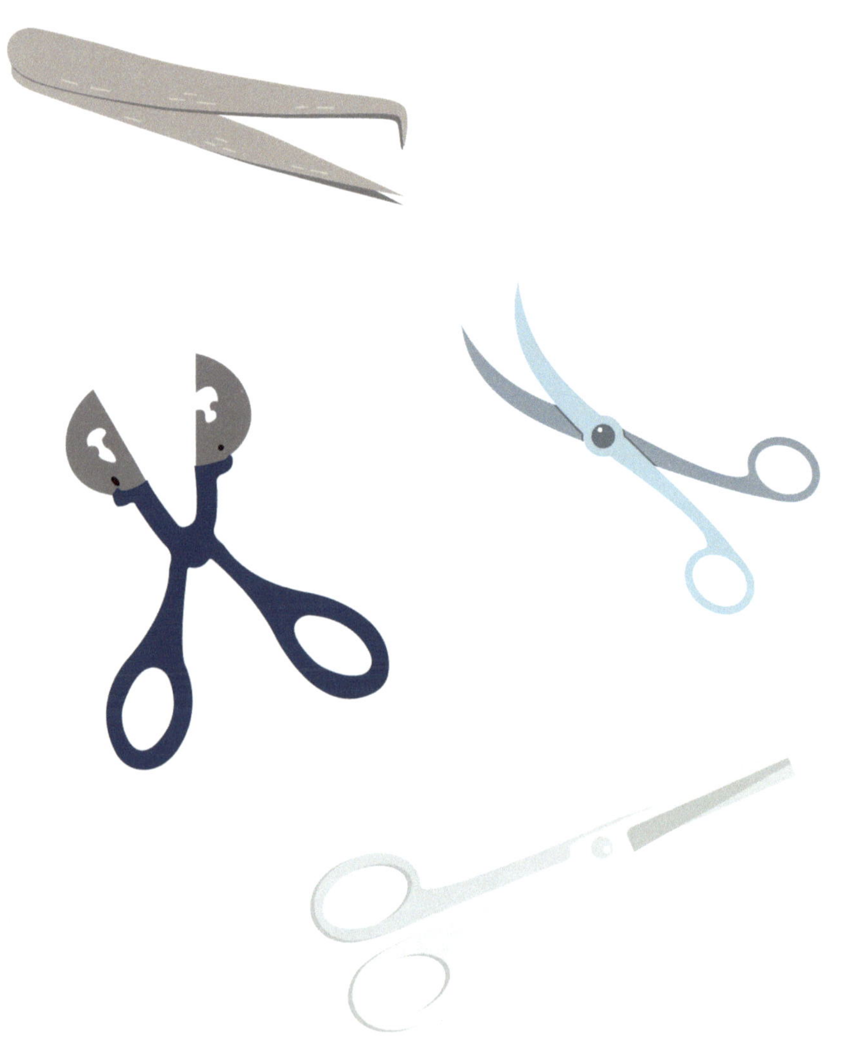

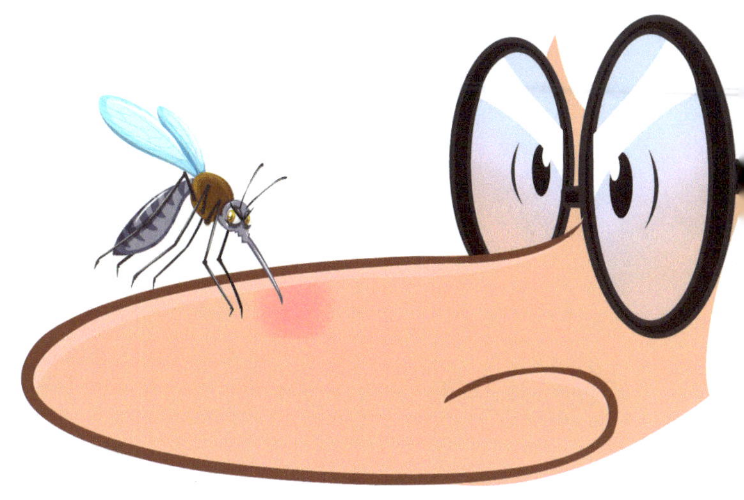

I can even catch them as they fly past my nose!

My favorite bugs are spiders!

My Grandma thinks spiders are scary!
I am not scared! Are you scared?

One day I watched an outdoor spider eat an indoor spider!

Yikes!

That was Gross!

I catch flies, rollypolly's, beetles, and ladybugs, too.

What about you?

Do not ever try to catch a wasp.
Whatever you do...

Did you know pincer bugs can fly?

They bite, too.

I caught a baby Praying Mantis the other day.

It was so small,

I could hardly see it at all.

There are so many bugs to find and catch.

I will try to catch them all!

Some get away but that is okay.

"I will try again another day".

I am a bug catcher because ...

I really like bugs... do you?

I hope you do, too.